First game at Forbes' Field
June 30, 1909

WAGNER
PITTSBURGH

WAGNER, PITTSBURG

WAGNER, PITTSBURG

Pennant Winners
PITTSBURG·B·B·CLUB
NATIONAL LEAGUE
1909

ALWAYS
BUY
THE
PITTSBURG
LEADER
DAILY
AND
SUNDAY

KING OF BALL PLAYERS

FOR ALL
AND THE
BEST
SPORT
NEWS
EVERYWHERE

WAGNER

WAGNER, Pittsburg Nat'L

"How about that!"

—Honus Wagner, after sharing a rousing story with friends or fans

WAGNER, PITTSBURG

IN JULY 2007 a rare baseball card
was sold at auction
for almost three million dollars.
The player on the card
was hatchet-faced, bandy-legged,
and arguably the most famous shortstop
baseball has ever known.
His name was Honus Wagner.
This is his story.

To my boys: Adam, Jason and wee David. —JY

To my brother Sean, for all those games of catch,
and to my favorite Pittsburgh Pirates fans and
loving in-laws, Jim & Kaye. —JB

JANE YOLEN

Illustrated by

JIM BURKE

ALL STAR!

HONUS WAGNER *and the*

MOST FAMOUS BASEBALL

CARD EVER

PHILOMEL BOOKS • AN IMPRINT OF PENGUIN GROUP (USA) INC.

That story begins on February 24, 1874,
in Chartiers, Pennsylvania.
It starts in the poor section of town, in a house
that stood a line drive from the railroad yard.
The house was already crowded with family
by the time the fourth surviving Wagner son
came into the world.
Named Johannes Peter, he was not a beautiful child.
His legs looked like hunting bows.
His arms were long.
Later it would be said he could tie his shoes
without bending over.
He had a big nose and a large head.
But his mother, Katheryn, and father, Peter,
thought he was gorgeous.
They called him Hans
or, more often, Honus.

Chartiers was one of a number of
little towns near Pittsburgh,
all huddled around unpaved streets
as if the houses could be kept warm that way.
The skies were constantly darkened by smoke
from the city's many steel and iron mills.
Settled by hardworking German immigrants
like Katheryn and Peter Wagner,
the town would later be renamed Carnegie.
The Wagner children grew up
speaking both German and English.
Honus learned to read and write
in both languages
in a small Lutheran church school
that only went up to sixth grade.

After sixth grade, there was no more school
for boys like Honus and his brothers.
They followed their father into the mines,
walking along together before it was fully light
on the paths well worn by the leather shoes
of miners who came before them.
Work ran from dawn to dusk six days a week,
so they carried the meal pails
that Katheryn Wagner had packed for them.
When Honus was only twelve years old
he worked loading two tons of coal a day for 79 cents.
"A boy's pay," he called it.
He began to pack on muscle.
"It was hard work but good exercise,"
he would later tell a reporter.
A miner's son learned not to complain.

But the Wagners had Sundays off.
And Sundays, after church, they played baseball.
All the Wagner boys loved the sport.
Honus got to try out many different positions
on their family team, including pitcher.
And though his legs were bowed,
he could run faster than the rest,
like an arrow flying along the base paths.
His long arms helped him snag
even the streakingest line drive.
And after all those months loading coal,
he was strong for a boy.
In fact, he was as strong as many men.
Often the Wagners played well into the evening,
with only the gas streetlamps to give them light.

One time, Honus played on the Oregons,
a team of local twelve-year-olds.
He came up to bat in the ninth inning
with two outs and one man on,
his team trailing by one run.
Honus belted out a huge hit
that scorched into the outfield.
The crowd of miners and miners' sons
called out: "Run, boy, run!"
And he ran—oh, how he ran,
those bandy legs pumping,
his twelve-year-old heart thumping,
the cool wind blowing in his hair.
But the boy on base in front of him
was the slowest runner on the team.
Honus couldn't pass him or the boy would be out,
ending the game.
Instead, Honus picked him up,
slung him over his back,
and carried him all around the base paths.
When they were done, Honus dropped the boy
onto the brick they used for home plate.
Only then did Honus himself step on the brick,
winning the game.
How about that!

At sixteen, Honus joined the Mansfield semipro team.
He was 5'11" and nearly 200 pounds,
and already known for his bowed legs,
long arms, and great barrel chest.
He called his huge hands "scoops."
They seemed too large for his baseball glove.
He made his glove even smaller
by cutting out a hole where the palm was
and pulling out lots of the stuffing.
He said he could feel the ball better that way.
Any position that was open, he played.
Often he was at shortstop or in the outfield,
but sometimes he pitched. He didn't care.
He just plain loved the game.

Honus wanted to follow his big brother Al,
already a pro on a Steubenville team fifty miles away.
Al begged his manager to give Honus a tryout.
The gruff manager made things hard.
"He has to be here this afternoon by two o'clock."
The Wagners had no telephone, so Al sent a telegram.
Now, in those days fifty miles was a long ways away.
The next passenger train would bring Honus in too late.
But Honus wanted to try out so much, he made it happen—
by hopping a freight train, then running from there to the field.
He'd left home so fast, he'd come away
without a uniform or glove or spiked shoes.
When he borrowed his brother's spikes,
his big feet split them apart.
But barefooted, bareheaded, he pitched his way
onto the Steubenville team.
How about that!

That year Honus played with not one, but five different teams in three states trying to make a living in baseball.

That year his father broke an arm in the mines. Brother Charles lost his barbershop when the landlord stole his rent money.

Honus fell against a picket fence
and was badly gashed under his armpit.
And some rotten thief stole
five chickens from the family coop.
But Honus had found his stride in baseball.
He'd become known as a strong hitter, a fast runner,
and a keen observer of the other players.
His sweet temperament made the newspapers
call him "Old Reliable,"
though he was only twenty-two years old.
It was time—perhaps even past time—
to be discovered.

Ed Barrow, a baseball executive,
heard about the young Pennsylvania phenom.
One cold winter day, he tracked Honus down.
Honus, wearing a derby hat
with a chicken feather in the band,
was at the railroad tracks with friends
throwing chunks of coal at a railway hopper.
Simple to spot, he was the boy who never missed,
hitting the hopper with loud regular thunks.
Barrow called out to the boys.
Figuring him for a railroad cop,
they ran like the dickens.
It was easy to follow Honus, not so easy to catch him.
But Barrow eventually caught up,
and offered him a place on a Paterson, NJ, team.
His pay: $125 a month.
(The average *yearly* pay for a worker then was $439.)
Honus jumped at the chance.

Honus batted .349 his first season.
In his second season,
he was bettering that by thirty points
when he was sold off to Louisville,
a National League club.
Honus Wagner was in the big leagues!
Of course, the majors were not so major then.
There were only twelve teams
and the rosters were much shorter than today.
But it was where professional ball was played.
His first year in the majors, Honus batted .344.
The major leagues were called "rowdy ball" by some.
Fans in the stands often threw bottles, gloves and punches.
At a game in Philadelphia, angry fans attacked the umpire,
throwing bottles and cushions at him.
Honus rushed to his side,
and using his bat as a weapon,
hit away all the missiles.
He never missed.
How about that!

Joining the Pittsburgh Pirates in 1900, Honus won the
National League batting championship in
1900, 1903, 1904, 1906, 1907, 1908, 1909 and 1911.

In 1909 the Pirates made the World Series
against the Detroit Tigers
and won in seven games.
Honus set two records
with his odd windmilling run
and his strangely bowed legs
that looked like a large parenthesis.
He stole six bases altogether—
a record which stood for 58 years—
and three of them in one inning—
a record which still stands today.
It was said that mouthy Ty Cobb
called Honus names in that series,
and that in return Honus tagged Cobb
so hard, right in the face during one game,
it loosened several of his teeth.
But both stars denied this ever happened.
Indeed, a play-by-play of the game proves
Honus never tagged Cobb at second at all.
But the legend persists.
How about that!

Honus had more home runs, RBIs, doubles, triples;
he had more steals; and he played in more games
than any other player in the National League.
Clearly he was a great baseball player . . .
some say the *greatest* baseball player ever.
And he did it all without drugs
or fancy training programs
or million-dollar incentives—
just for the pure love of the game.

Honus's fans—young and old—
collected everything about their hero,
like the Colgan Chewing Gum ad
in *The Saturday Evening Post.*
He even had his own baseball card,
until he realized it was sold in cigarette packs.
Since Honus did not smoke
and he worried about his young fans,
he had the card pulled off the market,
saying that it gave them
the wrong idea about cigarettes.
Still, a small number of the cards
had already gotten to the public.
However, they were very rare,
and in the years ahead, individual cards
would be extremely valuable.

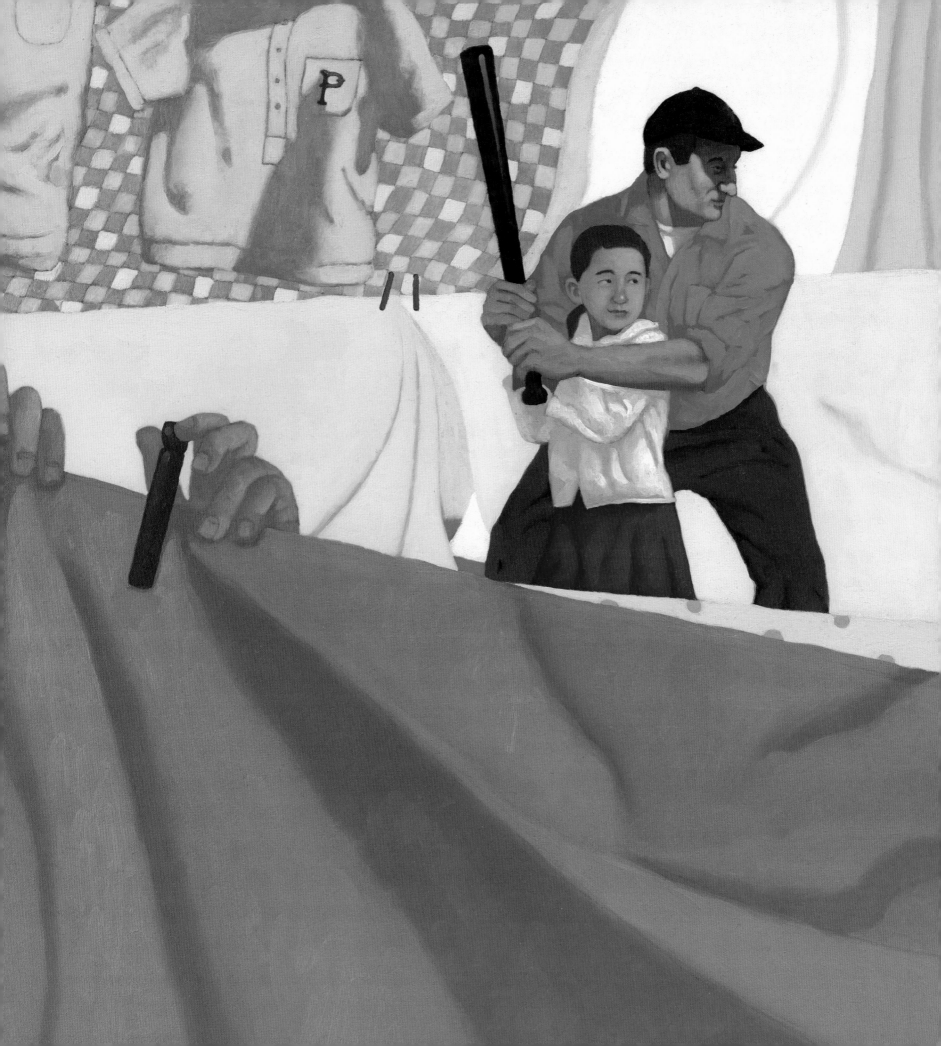

Honus played 21 seasons of major league baseball
before he had the courage
to ask the woman he loved to marry him.
They had two girls—Betty and Virginia.
Honus called them "my two boys,"
and taught them to play the game he loved.
He hunted, fished, played some basketball,
and helped organize a small baseball league.
But he missed the hurly-burly, the screams of the crowd,
the dust from a sliding steal curling up into his nose,
the thwacking sound of a ball hitting his glove.
So he rejoined the Pittsburgh Pirates—as a coach.
And in 1936 when the Baseball Hall of Fame was established,
Honus Wagner, the bandy-legged son of German immigrants,
was one of the first five men inducted.
How about that!

ARTIST'S NOTE

I have loved baseball, it seems, all of my life, from neighborhood pickup games to Little League to Red Sox games. One of my first memories of baseball is at Fenway Park, cheering for Jim Rice chasing down flies to left and joining in the wave when Carl "Yaz" Yastrzemski got up to bat. Over time I grew intrigued with some of the all-time legends, like Ted Williams, whom I will always remember meeting when I was a young boy. What was it that made such players so legendary? Was it their batting, fielding, or speed? Recently, I discovered Honus Wagner, maybe the greatest of the great in all areas of the game. You can imagine my absolute pleasure in researching such a legend for this book.

It was almost as if I were tracking the real Honus down. I visited and photographed his childhood home in Carnegie, Pennsylvania, as well as the home he later had built in the Library Hill section of Carnegie. Though Honus hadn't lived there since 1955, I was thrilled to see "JW" (Johannes Wagner) still carved on the doorbell plaque. I wondered how many fans rang that bell for an autograph of the old slugger.

The *Mona Lisa* of baseball cards, the famous T206, fascinates me. In tracking information about it, I contacted authors, biographers, sports reporters, historians, librarians, museums, auction houses and collectors. I found out that Swedish immigrant Carl J. Horner took the photograph of Honus that was used on the card. In his busy Boston studio he captured not only the timeless image of Honus, but the images of Ty Cobb, Walter Johnson and "Nuf Ced" McGreevy. He must have loved baseball too.

The most wonderful moment for me, though, was discovering the only existing Honus Wagner game-used bat (shown in the endpapers), which I found in the most prized private baseball collection, in Denver, Colorado. I actually held it my hands, and I thought of the old-time grip Honus used, hands spread apart—a grip Ty Cobb used too. What a moment that was.

Had Honus been told that his amazing life story from coal mines to baseball diamonds would finally be shared with children as well as adults, he would have been pleased. He always liked children. Perhaps the news would have been music to his ears, like Forbes Field packed to the rafters, the crowd on its feet, chanting *Hon-us, Hon-us, Hon-us*—this book is my cheer for the great man!

Jim Burke

A tremendous thank you to Marshall Fogel for generously sharing his landmark baseball collection, and to Doug Allen from Legendary Auctions for access to the famous T206 Wagner card. Thank you also to Rob Lifson at REA Sports for sharing his incredible archive of Honus Wagner baseball cards. A special thanks to the following: David Rudd Cycleback, Dick Price at the Senator John Heinz History Center, Michael O'Keefe, Frank Ceresi, Dennis DeValeria and Jeanne Burke DeValeria, authors of *Honus Wagner: A Biography*, Tim Wiles and John Horne at the National Baseball Hall of Fame in Cooperstown, and to Clare Anne Withers at the University of Pittsburgh Library.

Patricia Lee Gauch, Editor

PHILOMEL BOOKS
A division of Penguin Young Readers Group.
Published by The Penguin Group.
Penguin Group (USA) Inc., 375 Hudson Street, New York, NY 10014, U.S.A.
Penguin Group (Canada), 90 Eglinton Avenue East, Suite 700, Toronto, Ontario M4P 2Y3, Canada
(a division of Pearson Penguin Canada Inc.).
Penguin Books Ltd, 80 Strand, London WC2R 0RL, England.
Penguin Ireland, 25 St. Stephen's Green, Dublin 2, Ireland (a division of Penguin Books Ltd).
Penguin Group (Australia), 250 Camberwell Road, Camberwell, Victoria 3124, Australia (a division of Pearson Australia Group Pty Ltd).
Penguin Books India Pvt Ltd, 11 Community Centre, Panchsheel Park, New Delhi - 110 017, India.
Penguin Group (NZ), 67 Apollo Drive, Rosedale, North Shore 0632, New Zealand (a division of Pearson New Zealand Ltd).
Penguin Books (South Africa) (Pty) Ltd, 24 Sturdee Avenue, Rosebank, Johannesburg 2196, South Africa.
Penguin Books Ltd, Registered Offices: 80 Strand, London WC2R 0RL, England.

Published simultaneously in Canada.   Manufactured in China by South China Printing Co. Ltd.   Design by Semadar Megged.
Text set in 14-point Apolline.   The paintings for this book were created in oil on board.
Library of Congress Cataloging-in-Publication Data
Yolen, Jane.   All star! : Honus Wagner and the most famous baseball card ever / Jane Yolen ; illustrated by Jim Burke.   p. cm.
1. Wagner, Honus, 1874–1955—Juvenile literature. 2. Baseball players—United States—Biography—Juvenile literature. 3. Pittsburgh Pirates (Baseball team)—Juvenile literature. 4. Baseball cards—Collectors and collecting—United States—Juvenile literature. I. Burke, Jim. II. Title.
GV865.W33Y65 2010   796.357092—dc22   [B]   2009015066
ISBN 978-0-399-24661-6
7 9 10 8 6

PAT'S MARK
J. Hans Wagner
REG. U.S. PAT. OFF.

John H Wagner Nov 15–10
Pittsburg
B.B. Club
Short Stop

Pittsburgh for World Champions
JOHN HONUS WAGNER
for SHERIFF
Election, Nov. 3, 1925

Boston vs. Pittsburg
7
Grand Stand
RAIN CHECK
VOID AFTER
5 INNINGS ARE PLAYED

PITTSBURG

OUR PROTECTION
AGAINST LOSS
WAGNER

WAGNER
(PITTSBURGH NATIONALS)

Wagner, s.s. Pitts...

SUPPLEMENT TO The Sporting News, ST. LOUIS, SEPT. 29, 1909
HONUS WAGNER
Pittsburg National League

WAGNER

Wagner, s.s. Pittsburg Nat'l

HANS WAGNER
PITTSBURG